The Cartographer's Tongue

This book was supported by a grant from
the Greenwall Fund of the Academy of American Poets.

THE CARTOGRAPHER'S TONGUE
POEMS OF THE WORLD

SUSAN RICH

WHITE PINE PRESS • BUFFALO, NEW YORK

WHITE PINE PRESS
P.O. Box 236, Buffalo, New York 14201
www.whitepine.org

ACKNOWLEDGMENTS: Acknowledgment and thanks are made to the following journals in which some of these poems first appeared: *Alaska Quarterly Review,* "The Myth of the Perfect Move," "Traveling the Map." *Ariel: An International Review of Literature in English,* "Sarajevo."(Canada) *The Bellingham Review,* "Men at Work." *Bridges,* "The Woman With a Hole in the Middle of Her Face." *The Christian Science Monitor,* "In the Language of Maps." *DoubleTake,* "Spring Break." *Glimmer Train,* "In Search of Alternative Endings." *Gulf Stream,* "The Palmist." *Harvard Magazine,* "Tuareg Tea Ceremony." *Hedgebrook Journal,* "1959," "Muted Gold," "Whatever Happened to the Bodies..." *Kotaz,* "Oslobojenje" (South Africa) *Maryland Poetry Review,* "La Verbena Cemetery." *Mercator's World,* "How to Read a Map." *The Massachusetts Review,* "Love in the Time of AIDS." *New Contrast,* "Atopos: Without Place," "The Exact Moment." (South Africa) *New Coin,* "Early Morning Weather." (South Africa) *Pacifica Magazine,* "Flames." *Poet Lore,* "Green Street Grill." *Salamander,* "Train Travel," "Lessons in the Desert." *Santa Barbara Review,* "Lost By Way of Tchin-Tabarden," "The Wall," "Wendy." *Sarasota Poetry Review,* "Edgelight," "Nocturne," "Leaving Sarajevo." *Sojourner,* "The Place." *Soundings East,* "Haiti." *South Coast Poetry Journal,* "The Beggars." *Southern Humanities Review,* "The Scent of Gasoline." *Southern Poetry Review,* "The Mapparium," "Nomadic Life." *Texas Observer,* "Filigree of the Familiar."

I am grateful to the Blue Mountain Center, Cottages at Hedgebrook, Cummington Community of the Arts, the Millay Colony for the Arts, and the Wurlitzer Foundation for residencies which supported the completion of this work.

Innumerable thanks are due to the following people: Pamela Alexander, Carli Coetzee, Garrett Hongo, Barbara Helfgott Hyett, Ingrid de Kok, Jennifer Markell, Linda Pastan, Ruby Rich, Hilary Sallick, Katelyn Hibbard, Rustum Kozain, and Peter Wallace.

Special thanks also to Peter Ogura and the students of the Black Sun Poetry of Place workshops who have fortified me with strength and delight.

Book design: Elaine LaMattina

Third Printing

Cover image: "Map of the Ocean Floor" by Marie Thorpe.
Used by gracious permission of the British Library.

Printed and bound in the United States of America

Library of Congress Cataloging-in-Publication Data
Rich, Susan, 1959–
The cartographer's tongue : poems of the world / Susan Rich
p. cm.
ISBN 1-893996-06-9   (alk. paper)
I. Voyages and travels—Poetry. 2. Travel—Poetry. I. Title
PS3568.C38 2000
811'.54—dc21   99–044072
CIP

In Memory
Abraham and Lillian Rich

EXPLORATIONS

PARTS OF A GLOBE

MUTED GOLD

I want strong peace and delight, the wild good.
—Muriel Rukeyser

EXPLORATIONS

Lost By Way of Tchin-Tabarden

Republic of Niger

Nomads are said to know their way by an exact spot in the sky,
the touch of sand to their fingers, granules on the tongue.

But sometimes a system breaks down. I witness a shift of light,
study the irregular shadings of dunes. Why am I traveling

this road to Zinder, where really there is no road? No service station
at this checkpoint, just one *commercant* hawking *Fanta*

in gangrene hues. *C'est formidable!* he gestures—staring ahead
over a pyramid of foreign orange juice.

In the desert life is distilled to an angle of wind, camel droppings,
salted food. How long has this man been here, how long

can I stay contemplating a route home?
It's so easy to get lost and disappear, die of thirst and longing

as the Sultan's three wives did last year. Found in their Mercedes,
the chauffeur at the wheel, how did they fail to return home

to Ágadez, retrace a landscape they'd always believed?
No cross-streets, no broken yellow lines; I feel relief at the abandonment

of my own geography. I know there's no surveyor but want to imagine
the aerial map that will send me above flame trees, snaking

through knots of basalt. I'll mark the exact site for a lean-to,
where the wind and dust travel easily along my skin,

and I'm no longer satiated by the scent of gasoline. I'll arrive there
out of balance, untaught; ready for something called home.

Tuareg Tea Ceremony

In the desert men drink shots
of heavily sugared green tea.
It's men's work to pour and serve
three rounds of *chi*—for life,
for friends, and the heart's
sweet anticipation.
The Tuareg wear indigo turbans, robes the color
of sandstorms and scrub brush,
their high cheekbones unchecked by wind-torn cloth.
Achmad slides a spoon of jagged sugar
to his covered lower lip, exposes his mouth
wet and dark and sweet,—a gesture
that's meant to be seen. Relaxed on one elbow,
leaning their profiles into shadow and flame,
the men chat about women
or camels—as if the evening were poised,
the moment ready
to be itself in a photo proof.
By the fire, long and slender bodies
choose angles to emphasize the bend of light.
A woman's eyes journey along one covered thigh,
down a slope of calf and
resolve in perfect ankle.
Dari covets her face,
works mercilessly with his well-trained
and unambiguous grin.
Under the teapot two twigs
criss-cross. The men calmly fan them,
use the back of a sandal, a scrap of animal hide,
insistent that the flame stays alive,
burns hot and slow.
These men of domesticity and fire

eyes underlined in blue kohl—
are serious about the ceremony of tea.
As I am in stitching sorrow to desire.
Saidou drops his veil to drink,
then passes the sweet wet leaves
to the younger boys and they eat.

HAITI

It's 4 a.m. on her birthday
as she prepares for morning mass
wanting the luck
early prayers are said to bring.

Today she's turning sixteen
and the only one awake.
She brushes her hair back, drawing
it into a braid, puts in the silver earrings
tiny as insect eyes, and turns to admire
the curve of her legs in silk stockings.

She spies her brother's jacket
lifts it from the hook, singing under her breath.
The day is fine. The breeze feels cool along
the edge of her skin. She walks out onto the porch.
A shadow blocks her way down the stairs,
a body propped against bougainvillea
rigid against clay pots.

Here is a gift from the Ton Ton Macoute,
someone's brought Papa home.
A note pinned to his collar like a caption
she writes for her scrapbook. The face is
swollen, the soles of the feet burnt,
the lips one long purple bruise.
This family has 24 hours to leave.

There are no words to remember,
no beginning or end to this day.
Her mother puts them on the boat,
nodding good-bye from the dock,
I will join you.
The girl wonders when they became flecks
of glass, bits of color thrown out to sea.

She listens to the priest bless their voyage,
wondering at the words *asylum seekers*, doesn't know
she is one of ten thousand faces, that those like her
are not believed, are sent home, followed, and will leave

again. She watches her mother turn into the horizon.

THE MAPPARIUM

Boston, Massachusetts

In geography class we learn the world
of oceans, continents, and poles. We race
our fingers over mountain ranges and touch
rivers lightly with felt-tip markers. Deserts, islands,
and peninsulas tumble raw and awkward
off our tongues. *Kalahari, Sumatra, Arabia.*

We visit the Mapparium on a field trip.
A made-up word we learn
for the place where the world resides.
We clamor in with falling socks and high octave squeals
Palermo, Kabul, Shanghai,
exploring the globe, crossing its circumference we take flight
touch down on the see-through bridge.

The earth as it was, a time called 1932
stays in a room—retracts our breath,
our lives—makes history into color and light.
We look up at the Baltics, see *Lithuania, Latvia, Estonia,*
lands my grandmother left. Sixteen
and wanting the world.

I want to stay inside this world, memorize
the pattern of blue that conceals
the origins of every sea. A wave
hitting stone is the sound my voice leaves
as a pledge of return on the glass.
Feet to Antarctica, arms outstretched
like beacons toward Brazil;
I'll take this globe as my own.

SPRING BREAK

Peace Corps, Niger

It's a universal business that's brought them here,
into the night outside Agadez, into the ragged trimmings of light.

Past lean-tos of plaited mats, past fires that flare in an unfamiliar code
we follow these Wodaabe men—excited, raw nerved, enthralled.

What do they make of *les Mademoiselles Américaine* folded in dresses
as formless as millet sacks, skin the color of crusted goat cheese?

Do they mock Belinda's rosary of facts on Nigerien venereal disease,
laugh at Beverly's blue-inked notes: *A Chat with Nomadic Chiefs?*

Lives away from the *cas de passage,* from the signposts and streets
of a set geography, we've been invited for tea and mangoes—

to breathe in the wood smoke that will linger on our clothes,
mix with the unmistakable sweet hum of the body.

Along the bench one of us, one of them, our heads bent back
to hoard the sky as the stars throw themselves into arcs

of persistent flight. Dari stretches his elegant limbs
and I discover fingertips on my thigh, an arm nestled against my ribs.

The men know the art of insinuation, know how to penetrate a woman
with their eyes, hold her beyond the palm of conversation,

no deception save desire. My thumbs hook into the edge of my sleeves,
but I'm just along for the view—for the desert scent of truck exhaust
and jasmine,

hibiscus with a tinge of extremity. *Il n'y as pas d'etoiles chez vous?* Dari asks
lifting his lashes to a bottle of Visine. His lipstick glistening, gold make-up

marking the rise of high-boned cheeks. Conversation fades
and I admire my date's slim hips, his winged shoulders,

poised, inviting. But too much memory offends. To him this is nothing new,
only a chance to see if it's true that Peace Corps girls will do *presque tout.*

Their offer it seems almost impolite to refuse, *nous sommes trois et trois,*
but that's what I and Belinda and Beverly choose—we say no to pleasure,

to pairing off behind sand dunes. Say no to foreign hand
stitched robes, to anything we wouldn't know how to undo.

ATOPOS: WITHOUT PLACE

Kitchen pans tumble,
the medicine cabinet shakes.
You are nine. And the memory
is how you escape.
Airplanes soar over,
and well into the neighborhood.
Fireworks pop along the grocer's roof,
and across from your window   Alta,
the baker's wife, combs through debris
rescuing half-moons, marzipan, angel cake;
dusting off each one gently,
until a soldier drags her away.

     •

Atrocity is such a luscious word,
delicate, ebullient, pure.
The *ting* glass makes as it shatters
against glass; the timbre of a whimper
arcing upwards to a shriek   —then broken
by the taste   of an officer's soiled sock.
Atrocity: the way a woman knows
to mask her face when she discovers
her husband's severed head
wrapped in cellophane,
blood-caked at the garden gate.

     •

Our family owned a white Toyota,   ate dinner
in French restaurants, *coq au vin* and *saucisson*.
And when the TV camera showed live footage
of Zimbabwe,   El Salvador,   the young Chinese—
we flipped the channel,   in Bosnia,   in peace.
We have lost the picture of ourselves.
We've lived enough   to lose, to lose again,
no longer evoking who we ought to have been.
We're tired of running. *We take our children*
and walk toward silence.

●

Home is a makeshift tent of sticks and blankets.
If I grow up, I want to be a doctor,
the daughter says, *I'll operate on soldiers.*
Home is a camp, a lean-to, anonymous snores. *Would you*
have patience with psychiatrists? We refuse all journalists.
The women space themselves into squadrons of nine:
a row of knit one, purl;   grasp the yarn firmly,
circle over,   the skein unwinds but comes back
as gloves or hats.   The hands articulating
what the body knows: pull the thread, click the needles,
the story will unfold, translate as yours, translate to mine.

THE WOMAN WITH A HOLE IN THE MIDDLE OF HER FACE

Republic of Niger

She begs in the bus station
with no nose at all, just one black hole
expanding where her nostrils used to breathe.

Two front teeth jut out
at fancy angles, extend
from inside wet-flesh cheeks.

The woman doesn't speak
or acknowledge other lepers,
but sits in the shade of a thorn tree

distancing herself from children
who use her, hovering (none too close),
for their own economy. Increased disease

means more water, *tsadakah,* meat.
She works minus the comfort of equipment,
no carved-out gourd or favorite cup;

the coins her only interaction
with another, fingers forced
for half an instant—recoil

on to hers. Does pain live more
in the fragments than the whole?
The smell of desert dust, of skin

edged with sweat—what
does she miss the most?
What is it to live inside the body,

to reside in a geography of pain;
afraid of what sight desires
but is unprepared to see?

Atrocity. The woman
with no nose did honorably,
disfigurement translated

to generous pay.
Everyone bypassing experience
to persuade her to move away.

The Myth of the Perfect Move

I moved in a dazzling black taxi,
on the back of an open pick-up truck.

By special delivery and once in the middle
of the night before the concierge came back.

I moved by air taking comfort
in the layers of sky above cloud, watched

as my life rose above the traffic flow
over an illuminated baseball diamond.

My addresses piled up like images on a TV screen
from *St. George's Quay* to *Leith Walk*

along the *Calthorpe Close,* I oriented
myself with a river, an Italian rooming house.

I moved instead of longing, instead
of imagining the Sphinx at daybreak

when the stones awake and purr
glad to be alone.

And I searched to forego belonging
like a Bedouin who leaves her home

hung inside a desert tree
knowing it does not really matter

if the branches are bare when she returns,
if she decides, to come back this way again.

NOMADIC LIFE

Republic of Niger

When I come back with the cups of tea
the sugar bowl has been emptied,
my imported M&Ms—
gone. Flies stretch their legs
search, then spiral
in a dust storm of light.
Aisha sits solemn in afternoon heat
examines the inside of ice cubes
questions what makes water
strong or weak.
We invent common words between us,
point at the refrigerator door,
the photograph of ferns rising out of snow
the last volunteer left behind.
I'd like to trade with her
my typewriter keys
for the way she navigates the desert
reads the coordinates of sand.
I want to know as Aisha knows
when it's time to follow
the ambivalent line of landscape
keep faith in dunes that disappear.
By evening when she tastes
my color-coated chocolates
shares them with her friends
we both will recall the nomad
the other woman
we each might have been.

In the Language of Maps

The mapmaker is measuring the earth,
seeking the accurate. She knows her projection
must distort the geography of the world.
Tracing distance and direction
on parchment, paper, or cloth;
she chooses the one which best suits her purpose.
She'll work to ensure that Denver stays
its correct distance from Milan,
that the Nile finds its way to Lake Nasser.

Now she uses lasers and light beams.
She colors mountain ranges, rivers,
defines the depths of oceans. Longitude, latitude, the poles
at each end of the axis—she keeps ever steady.
The mapmaker consolidates her power.

She revises surface boundaries
for Germany and Yugoslavia;
draws borders around Eritrea, Namibia
and wonders this time, if her lines are exact.
Using familiar signposts and symbols as code,
the cartographer knows
it is her maps which form the images
in everyone else's mind. She knows
the language of maps is constantly changing.

THE WALL

"What superstition and fanaticism on every side.'
—Theodore Herzl

We Jews slip secrets inside cracked mortar
the flap of an envelope
half a postcard from home.

Call them prayers or wishes,
reasons why one must travel continents
to ask in-person
for advice or apology.

Here is the mailbox of God
where a woman walks backwards
after praying, never turning
her back to the wall.

Above her head tiny airplanes
originate explosions
scuttle across orchid blue sky
intent on their military exercise.

A hard light binds weathered stone
bleaches the guard-studded square,
where a neighborhood was razed in a night.
Mosques and homes. Mosques and homes.

LESSONS IN THE DESERT

for Sa-a

The Wodaabe aren't allowed to read
or write their names
in spiral bound notebooks
as I taught the boy to do.
After allowing our visits for months,
friendship propagating like a stubborn weed,
they accepted his forays into the peculiar,
the way of life inside my home.

How he played the music
imprisoned in a silver box,
stood in streams of water
falling from a ceiling pipe,
and shared peanut sauce spread on bread
instead of as he was used to.

But it was this word he'd learned to write,
the name which meant the lucky one,
Sa-a, that made them whip the bridge
of his nose, the lashes and soft lids
as if to keep his eyes shut tight,

closed against schools of any sort—
and other things nomads had no use for.
Survival meant to keep him
from slipping away,
from getting lost in the lines of the page.

THE TOUGHEST JOB

Republic of Niger

My students believe in ready answers,
the elegance of the equation. They know where
Amina is going, whom Amadou will meet at the well.
Anyone can tell you it takes forty goats to buy a wife
and that only a Baccalaureate
burns paths through millet fields
to the tarmac of the Route Nationale.

The old man slaps the hubcap, gongs
it with his cane. Saidou and Moustapha shuffle in
exchanging wise guy grins. *Miss, please,*
may I marry your sister?
What do you think of Kaddafi? Is it true
that the Americans
put socks on their hands to keep warm?

The blackboards are covered
in cartographic shapes, craters and plateaus.
A spiral of fly-studded neon light,
a broken ceiling fan, buzz and whirl —
in each classroom.
What can my students learn?

To sit exams set up for failure;
master percentages and fractions
exacting how much income
Abduhl will never make—
though he's promoted through
Seconde, Premiere, Terminale.

Here in the Sahel boys dust wooden benches
with sun-bleached handkerchiefs, copy dictée
in dueling red and blue Bic.
My students snap their fingers together,
Miss, Miss, Miss, their arms set at right angles,
their heavy breath at my neck,
assume the answer is decipherable,
visible on my bronzed skin, my hair.

But I know that Amadou can only lose,
that although Amina will accurately measure
the distance from Madaroufa to Wisconsin,
name the properties of stars, she'll sell postage stamps
and telephone calls to foreigners
who taught her *instigate, obliterate, win*.

THE BEGGARS

Republic of Niger

The beggers are leper ladies who gossip and laugh
all day holding their tin bowls with two or three fingers,
the only ones they have. Dry and strong as desert plants
they work always together, nodding and smiling
whether coins fall against their silver containers or not.

Skin tough as old meat, eyes bright as well water
the women have been standing like question marks
against the post office wall and a little to the right,
longer than anyone can remember.

The Filigree of the Familiar

Gaza City, Gaza

Here, all the men wear mustaches
which decorate their faces
in soft curved designs.
Mornings they bring me tangerines,
faux French bread,
and the daily day-old news.

The mustaches shift in color, shape, and size
depending on the wishes of each man
to expose his better self; to project his own
combed landscape: a miniature scissors,
a mirror in his hand.
So many mustaches! Such strange lands!
Some thick as kitchen brooms,
smooth as the Negev sands; Ibrahim's
opaque as winter light
brushed from the rim of the moon.

In laundry rooms, in stairwells,
in cities, on continents, there are periscopes
and clocks, garbage cans and front door lights
that whisper shyly if we just stand still
a warrantee will be provided
with instructions for our lives:
how to settle for less, how not to grow old.

Do I leave to take a stand?
Or circle around the globe,
passport in hand to get away from the incessant
no-win scenes, the frantic filigree of the familiar
pressing like dead dreams inside my head?

And is it right that I speak of the women of Gaza
in their *hijabs* and long sleeves,
to imagine stories of their domestic breathing?
Must I turn away from Ram allah, Hebron,
the East Gate entryway? Decline sweet offers
from Yusef and Samir—
not dance at Omar's wedding
but keep my body alone?

But then, if I describe only what is already inscribed,
I'd never see the black man on my street
who sweeps with an imaginary broom,
never see the Indian Ocean
assert itself, then recede.

We move about the world
watching for signs of what we already know
is best; a parentheses of photographs to pause in,
an isolated palm-lined beach to rest.
And at what point do I become the souvenir?
A faceless history set in amber?

Must I write only of hometown corners
swan boats, street cars, Boston Harbor—
to stay in the odd intersections
New Englanders call squares?
And which house is the home where I remain?
Juggler Meadow Road or Edinburgh?
Devon Street or Chelsea?
Home or travel, and which is which
and whose choice is it to say?

And if home might be any dot on the map—
maybe the one which is furthest away,
then I'll find mine only with a telescope.
Somewhere there's a life with tethered satellite
linking the outbound voyage to the everyday.

PARTS OF A GLOBE

SARAJEVO

I have a taste for burnt, crusty things: food brittle and carboned to black,
houses where the Serb militia have been. I adore the hard surface,

the finality of things charred and distorted beyond belief,
the decaying corners of morning toast, a pie crust singed, scarred skin.

I've grown accustomed to jagged peaks, watching
for snipers where lonely hikers once streamed, wandering paths

with their tri-colored packs. Give me hospitals inscribed in shrapnel,
unlocked closets of abandoned, anonymous bones. Bring bouquets

for the market massacres; kiss back streets studded with the Sarajevo Rose.
Rest assured, knowing all is exactly as it seems:

bruised, recast, burnt-out, impaled—somehow cleansed; as I write only
of what I cannot leave, a body awakening in the contours of waste and disease.

TRAVELING THE MAP

Merida, Mexico

The map shows me my attempted life.
My finger finds *Cozumel*
starts on the exact spot, the turn in the road
the town at the top of the mountain where I began.
It travels a patch of Caribbean sea
the width of a thumbnail
and tries to remember

Villahermosa and *Ciudad del Carmen*
the extra day not spared
the waterfall there was no time for.
Names I can't pronounce
or find on timetables
still elude me. I retrace the lines
see *Hidalgo,* and rest with the statues of *Atlantis*.

A thick trail of highlighter follows me
from *Playa* to *Merida*
where birds travel by bus, their wings cut,
their eyes moving
toward the palm leaf covered houses
where each is to be devoured by morning
bones left to dry on a table.

A child's eyes stay on me and I pretend
I don't feel her naked stare.
A young drunk teeters
into my taxi, hangs his head out the window
and explains to the driver why a fantasy
orgy with the *gringa* is worth it.
How they can catapult my body further down the road.

On the map the states are shaped
like spirits
with callings all their own—
Oaxaca, Tabasco, Quintana Roo;
they promise me the brilliance
of escape,
the shimmer of sky at dusk.

HOW TO READ A MAP

The maps expose
seven continents, travel
through oceans, the mouths of rivers,
each transparent page overlapping

And drifting on to the next.
In which direction do islands face?
Sometimes I look for river
crossings, re-trace the *Strait*

Of Gibraltar, the *Gulf*
of Cadiz. Pencil points
and circles serve to locate me,
make visible the invisible

Boundaries of village, suburb,
coastal town.
Symbols of airports,
cross-stitch of railway tracks,

Connect me to moving things—
I go with explorers
and Bedouins, with men
who imagine just one path exists:

A precise route to meaning.
How to simplify a coastline,
erase a military sight?
In the migration charts left

On birch bark, maps carved on white
bone, on the silk of a
Chinese scarf, *Which culture
remains unmarked?*

I go toward peninsulas and glaciers,
inlets and islands and streams,
questioning the shapes and ellipses
of propaganda and artistry.

Early plans rendered on pottery shards
show land ripe for taxes,
for the mining of gold; for poxed
blankets and conquerors.

Now I search for Nubia and Persia,
Ladakh and Palestine;
admire the fine plates of color,
the small truths and shaded relief.

How to construct new cartographies?
I learn the mapmaker's legend
aware she cannot know
what's been smoothed over,

What we leave behind—
anymore than I.
What lies on the other side of the lake?
Hibiscus, qualia, space—

Arranging themselves
in frames of unknown stars,
elegant as cryptograms,
falling and unafraid.

La Verbena Cemetery

In Guatemala City
the dead are buried
in rented tombs
laid out like housing projects
for the afterlife.

Occupants are stacked
eight bodies high,
the family name inscribed
in erasable ink.
By each drawer a coffee can waits
for sweet peas and saint figurines.

Each year, the fee is charged
until surviving relatives
can no longer pay
for a place
so disarmingly safe.

And then what remains
of the body, a cracked skull
burned thighs—
rises up in yellow smoke rings
and the ashes of the departed
mix with the factory waste.

TAOSEÑO

Even the sun is different here:
more generous along its helioptrope horizon
and people, too,

shape their words more thoughtfully,
in sentences slower
than I've known before

as if language itself
is an impediment to knowing
what they know.

So much written in
the arrangement of blues
and browns: open mesas

and mountains the color
of worn skin;
everything breathing

in and pausing.
Morning as the magpies dive
and the sagebrush swings

itself into a silver-rimmed spring,
I walk away from *Avenue El Destino*,
leave *Calle Conquistador*,

and head toward the Morada;
past laundry lines of shining white shirts
and tenderly mended blue jeans,

to watch as the light
travels the length of this ruin
this place of silence and sheen.

—Taos, March 1999

THE WHEELCHAIR REPAIRMAN'S BRIDE
IMAGINES HER FIRST NIGHT

Republic of Niger

She wonders if she'll straddle him
in this wheelchair he's built.
Her eyes begin at the bridge of his nose,
travel lips,   the strength of chin,
along a developed line of clavicle.
She sees his shoulder blades curve
into brazen muscles. Admires the jut
of a diamond rib cage.
Glances further on,   then pauses
by his belt-clad slender hips.

Or could she grow bolder?
And stroke his feet
bent like melted silver,
twisted as a snake's embrace.
Massaging upwards
she'd press both palms,
and rub the skin
of chalk thin calves.

Just inside his thighs,
she'd keep stretching callused fingers,
her motions spiraling like spokes of light
coaxing the innocent muscle,
determined she could convince limbs
to become unparalyzed.
Her body balancing
the upper and lower worlds;
their skin igniting.

WHATEVER HAPPENED TO THE BODIES...

I listen to my radio not for music, but the news.
The Orthodox are out again behind the yellow lines,
They're scraping blood off sidewalks, limbs from city streets.

Whatever happened to the skin of memory?
Whatever happened to the elbows, kneecaps, teeth?
Whatever passes for tenderness only veils our disbelief.

I listen to Linda Gradstein as I Comet clean the kitchen sink.
Every scrap of flesh, every drop of blood, you try to get it, she repeats.
Behind my house the raku kiln is firing masks and beads.

Whatever happened to the bodies cut and maimed?
Whatever held the hand which lit the gas?
Whatever scenario we imagine, we miscast.

I listen ready to participate—scrubbing souls from Tel Aviv's streets.
Propel the senses to migrate beyond what I can think.
The prayers I'm meant to remember, the unutterable, the indistinct.

Whatever happened to the bodies without names?
Whatever became of people cannibalized, drowned, depraved?
Whatever moves us eventually moves away.

I listen to the neighbors in their yard:
Angel, Silver, Red, and Ma. I move
with concentrated ease, dusk is smothering the trees.

Whatever happens to the bodies still alive?
Whatever exuberance may they hold?
Whatever dies returns to be retold.

OSLOBODJENJE

Sarajevo, Bosnia

The first year of the siege
we changed sizes thirteen times,

no one expected to see
a paper come out of those flames.

Yes, we had losses.

The local correspondent in Zvornick,
our finance clerk traveling between offices.

Yet, on that last bus out of the city,
no one wanted to leave.

The paper migrated from yellow to blue to green.

There was just bread and paper,
and there were many days without bread.

GHAZAL FOR THE WOMAN FROM VITEZ

Vitez, Bosnia

It's the best watermelon in the world
but there's no way to say it in words.

She had squatted in the space for apples and pears
under the staircase, a year, beyond the place of words.

Now she comes back with tea, examines me closely,
my out-of-date phrase book, my mispronounced words.

I ask for the toilet and she shows me the bedrooms, bombed
by neighbors who should have known how to use words.

We walk out to her garden in late afternoon light,
survey squash plants and corn stalks, we re-enter words.

In Bosnian the tomato is called *paradise*, sweetness
transferred from some other country's words.

We drink rounds of whisky, call her sons on the phone
laughing because we have found a way out through words.

LEAVING SARAJEVO

The bus driver stops to pick plums
from an abandoned late summer garden,

the pale blue carrier bags pulled from his bed
where he sleeps underneath the bus.

All night we watch movies,
drink beer in the dark, cross borders

where Bosnians, Croats and Serbs
will read and re-read our passports,

our papers: the litmus test of war.
We travel Prijedor, Banja Luka, Tuzla,

toward an airport light of home;
past minefields and orchards

fueled by sweet Sarajevan plums
our hearts are no longer our own.

L'OISEAU BLEU

Segu, Mali

Did they make love that night
in the small cement room
the color of desert amber, blister beetles
covering the adjoining wall
with their streams of blister juices?
Was her body fueled
by others' tender limbs
twisting mechanically in cells
above and below—
The intermittent moan
of one-sided pleasure
the energy of pain. What is it
that a body needs
to remain alive?

A baobab tree finds its way
into the topography
of the brothel, studies
the glitterless bar—
disguises itself
as a spiraling staircase.
In harmony, young and old men
rise seamlessly, slip
francs into the palm of the bartender
pimp—then disappear
behind enduring women.
Scaling the enigmatic statue—a puzzle
of stairs or a ripening tree? They arrive
in off-kilter rooms
level with branches and leaves.

Is it inevitable
this mythology of desire?
A simple whoring
of the self? Was I the one
wholly in love? Tonight pursuing
memory—the she that grew up to be me?
Did they decipher the desert
uncover an absence of roads;
their fingers caressing the trigger of disaster
or by dumb luck—a sort of ecstasy?
Who could feel the future
where the world would break apart
spew boulders and burnt out roots
from beneath the skin?
One negating it had ever been
love after all, just—a—kind
of sweet mistake?

That night I listened
to the sound of spray
from one mildewed shower stall.
Water trickling along the corridor,
a tree branch banging
our tin door open, while men
rigorously rinsed their bodies—
as if a shower stall might absolve
our unbearable urges at all.

SCIENCE LESSONS

Our galaxy is a spiral
of rotating arms,
inescapable union of stars,
dust, and cloud.
The sun just one
of a billion,
the closest light we have
and what we see is only the surface.

·

Scientists say time is only imagined,
not actually linear, not fixed
on one indivisible course. What if
we could construct our lives
in sets of spiraling rings;
what if we could remember our future,
the silver anniversary enacted
before the kiss *I do*.

·

Is what is essential
invisible to the eye?
When bodies move
they rearrange pockets
in space,

influence time;
and time revises our bodies—
the aging shapes we take.

•

It takes eight minutes
for the sun
to arrive;
for light rays to reach
towards Earth.   What creates
luminosity,
in the space of zero
to   eight?

•

Why such analysis of starlight?
When temperatures rise high enough
the first stars
will appear.
Generations of stars
grazing comfortably,
on the decay of others.

•

Why care that each dies
isolated, uncoupled
but still lit?
Is it friction that unhooks
a falling star,
that makes a heart revolt

underneath its illuminated
landscape of skin?

•

Antares, Mimosa, Capella,
the composition of any star,
identical to that of a hydrogen bomb.
Outer layers peel away with heat and need;
ignite in smoke-filled blue light.
Sometimes stars swallow stars,
pull one to another in thankless relief;
all sugar and glide.

•

Emitting their last glimmer
of energy, losing gravitational
force, stars desolate
as we are arc
downward, careen like the dying
ship on course
into the heart's
inevitable divorce.

Stories

January thaw in the Berkshires, 4 a.m., and what I want
and what you say you want, is enormous and infinitesimal

as desire postponed in this studio, this barn, this fragment
of a night. *Tell me a story*, I say as you pace back and forth fully awake.

In this year of ninety-nine inches of snow, other guests
invisible in sleep, your body turns to face me, your voice

begins its breathless reckoning and at the nape of your neck,
silky and hot, you start to blush. The last night alone.

"On deck at night with a girl, it's her idea, she's almost seventeen.
He is twelve, tall for his age, uncommonly naive.

She takes him up to the bow, takes him and his corduroy pants
in the palm of one hand. Unbuckles him with the other.

It's winter break, his first sea voyage, his parents'
silver anniversary. Is this girl why it's called *a pleasure cruise*—

the words that the blond captain used as he welcomed
everyone aboard. He sees the girl's wide eyes,

concentrates on a plum-colored wart on the edge
of her chin. She pulls his fly.

And only then, then does she kiss him;
still keeping her place, her fingers slick

and sea-salted between his thighs.
It's his first time with a girl,

the first time and his body doesn't know
how to do the thing it's desperate to.

So she is doing everything, touching the tip
of his tongue with her own. Using all of her body

against his body: hips and shoulders and knees.
What does it feel like? Her voice a surprise,

his pleasure reigns him alone. Unfurls in the air
as he reaches the rhythms of another's touch,

another's dumb reprieve. *I wish you could
be inside, come inside.*

He has no idea what she means.
It's her that's brought them here, on top deck

on a night without stars. *Please!*
Her hand is moving faster now, he is moving

further away. The boy unfastens from the boat,
orbits unmoored through dark space;

quivers but tries to hold tight.
Come inside! But there's no inside any more—

he's out, unravelled, undone. She's licking her wrist,
the creamy drops of a bracelet chain he's made.

And then they hear it *yes!*, and another *yes!*
louder now—from the floor below. Sounds from home

from a Sunday afternoon match, a sudden score
re-play on the downstairs console TV.

His father's unmistakable roar and the wind
and the young woman crying out is someone he doesn't know."

Your turn, you say and slip off my sweater,
tell me a story.

.

But these are our stories, two people locked in the continuous
accumulation of snow. The sky tonight dim, apron-colored,

and the view from your window exposes a wet meadow,
the tree line beyond. Another night not to sleep but to listen;

to withhold touch as the mice run rings in the corner of the studio.
I'm inhabiting the inside between *before* and *after,* the open line

stretched as far as I can hold—though no telephones work
for your lover to call, no passable roads,

no reason for these boundaries of the skin.
Another glass of red wine and my turn begins:

"You will be telling me over veal parmesan and a side of fries
how you'll undress me, undo my blouse and taste the salt

of hip and breast until you reach the stubborn cleft of my chin.
And next when we meet in the afternoon light, I'll still want the V

where your shirt frames your chest, the Adam's apple
sliding, darting, not revealing a thing—while you go

on talking; taking off my heels, rippling my stockings
from the inside of my thighs, enraptured

with description; blushing while the waitress pours more coffee.
Is everything all right? she'll ask, her apron stained

with chicken fat, parsley flakes, red things. Your voice only
seconds ago wishing for the strength to touch me again.

I could stay like this all evening, my would-be lover
adorning me in untethered tones and phrases until

I'm no longer there, just wary of the tables
as you tumble us above the ceiling fans in irresistible delight;

our real world bodies anchored inside a blue booth,
castaway in this territory we can't rescue."

Your shirt, I say and you strip off; arching
your fingertips as if for emphasis along my leg.

As if shots of light had not already begun
their steady rising into the bruised sky,

as if each door frame were not yet straining beneath
the surprise of excessive snow.

What does this feel like, you say
as if this cleaving, this consciousness, this barn,

had somewhere to go.

THE PALMIST

She touches a stranger's hand, turns it into the light.
Examines the spacing of fingers, the arc of his thumb,
the way the head line forks towards Upper Mars.
She takes in the whole from the curve of his wrist
to the pink inside the nails. She learns the language of his hand.

She measures flexibility, admires the sculpture of knuckles,
the relationship of flesh to bones. In the islands, branches, stars
meaning unfolds. Words she cannot anticipate
come from her lips. She knows more than she tells.

Every hand she reads is a map she gets to travel,
a master plan of past and potential lives.
She touches the mounts, then fingers the chains—
discovers another's journey and holds on.

She knows the Kabbalah of the Jews, the Brahmin's Hindu Vedas.
She knows nothing is written until we write it
and rewrite it again, that it's desire that alters destiny
that all of our lines will change.

NOCTURNE

I take my place in the insomniac's village,
4 a.m. blue gum trees in the yard.

Hello darlin' you tell me, only it's over
and out through the ether,

letters shadowed against a lighted screen.

In unheated rooms, the blue shutters calm,
I hold faith in illuminated signs,

pomegranates, stellae,
a double-knot of miracles in the street.

What do Bedouins believe?

On continents not our own,
we test our skin along the silences

of grief, the ordinariness of townships,
truth commissions, Clifton beach.

I send you no postcards, no
subject headers, just messages

of *pineapples, feathers, and shells.*

With dots and arrows we tell
stories larger than ourselves.

5:15 and the sky is winter green.

Pray for me.

In Cape Town, in Jerusalem,
we light candles,

wash our hands, salt and tear
the bread; the rituals

for a hungry place
I can't locate to conceal.

Come, let us eat with angels.

Let's toast the allure of
unattainability, the sweet ruin,

a romance never-to-be.

How will this country answer you?

With salvaged alphabets and song

we forage words, tracking
sibilants or sonorants of speech:

songololo, shimmer, orisons.

Another night without sleep.

Which research would you send me,
which holography for your belief?

I picture you opening high windows,
on the outskirts of olive groves,

a *tzaddik* raising holy sparks
along Jerusalem's morning streets.

Listen, here's the double note
of dove call: the somnambulist's psalm

with a second, private keening.

7 a.m., the blue gums edge-lit,
almost honed, almost revealing.

WENDY IN THE '90S

> "Wendy, Wendy when you are sleeping in your silly bed
> you might be flying about with me saying funny things
> to the stars. Wendy," he said, "how we should all
> respect you."   —Peter Pan

This time she would know better.
There would be no sewing shadows
mending the boys' tails, hot afternoons
cooking alligator, skinning
the pirates for stew.
She'd rather walk the plank.
Why would she go with him?
After the storytelling
windows open to the night
she would not be fooled by promises
of fairy dust or tempted with the offer
of mothering lost boys.
No patience with false Romance
she'd go only for the flying—
a movement like magnets to the stars.
Second to the right
and straight on till morning.
Air travel would win her over.
Energized, she'd start a union
for the mermaids
find counseling for Peter
and be off again.
She'd move above volcanoes, investigate
a tangle of clouds.
And then like the pilot resisting
the runway home, she'd hold her breath
and offer up this
pleasure—the telling
of the journey out alone.

TRAIN TRAVEL

Early morning rises off the fields.
Poplars in the shape of slender fans

open in rows like clothespins on a line.
More fields dense and green

a farm house, a villa,
the sweet stench of cattle.

One shack elongates in the wind
as railway speed awakens shape to movement

tracks sway left to right and back
again in a trick of double vision.

Everything is an echo
of the thing it thinks it is.

A man stares at rows of wheat
or admires his reflection

the honey-colored stems or the way the cheekbones
hollow as he takes in smoke and holds it.

Windows frame us, divide
passengers from a land of light

time alters with a simple switch,
a lever. I feel the air jump outside

as the other train approaches, rumbles closer
as if exploding rocks from underground.

And for a moment it's too close
yet racing by—an arc of industrial light,

it vanishes in to the opposite direction;
the journey's other journey, the one I travel to find.

And I wonder where my other self is bound for,
where in the end are the worlds we leave behind.

ON PHOTOGRAPHING THE NATIONAL LIBRARY

Sarajevo, Bosnia

Dramatic staircases leading nowhere.
Now nothing is pretty here.

A man in white overalls leans over
his wheelbarrow.

He nods his okay and we walk
through the doorway.

Cracked brick and splinters of stone.

What does a picture reclaim
of this simple province of pain?

Jagged edges of empty frames.

Fractures of green and blue
where once lived stained glass windows.

Does it really matter,
whether we photograph the disaster?

The man beckons with broken finger,
signals for the camera to flash towards him.

He grins and brings his friends,
soon the friends are laughing.

Books and papers bombed away.

Dobra, they tell me, *dobra*.
The photograph is good, the photo is okay.

In the swirl of a
thumbprint, one fossilized leaf,

on surfaces stenciled and stained; even here,
some rubbing of the unreal remains.

In Our Name

Inside this room we don't come to: the sizzle and spit
as of fat in a pan, a sweet-heavy smell
of flesh in flames, and two exhaust fans turning

toward a man whose hair on his left leg
and head have been shaved,
a diaper pinned in the waist of his jeans.

No prayers, no words, will he slip
in his hands; only the fingers
can legally burn into blue smithereens.

Here is the soft mauve cloth he'll wear
which will hide the human face
when the veins push out of his molting skin

like glass ridges on a jar or vase.
Let this chair mark the spot
where his heart shudders, then pops

in accordance with Florida law.
Here, stand in this room
with no view of the sea, meet the warden

the Imam, the Rabbi, the Priest.
See the doctor who shines a light in the eye
of a man when he's three minutes dead.

Here in a room, with a switch on a wall,
is one citizen paid always in cash—assuring us
the nightmares he has may never be publicly shared.

FLAMES

The Tarot reader told me what to do,
her instructions were to write
then burn the pages. Flames
for the red hot mouths of lovers,
flames for the unsaid.
I walk to the stationers,
find fuchsia and chartreuse papers
meant to lift a man away.

Flames for the words that won't be read.
Flames for a final salve.
I pour rubbing alcohol into a bowl—
douse one sheet at a time,
like French toast soaked in yellow froth;
crushed cinnamon, raw eggs.

Everything happening here on this stove top.
Bright colors bought just for this
to burn him out of the body.
Flames for the girl who was lost, flames
for the young man from France.
From paper to ash the stationary explodes
like fireworks arced into the sky;
hot light in silver and indigo
spark like figures burned by chance.

It was my fourteenth week when he asked me
to exit his country, said to send him
the infant as soon as it was born. As soon
as it could travel alone. (*By six months*
the stewardess demurely said.)

Burn whole sentences and memories
from the brain. What I can't forget
I can burn. Flames for this extra-fine felt tip;
flames for the years *say it* obsessed.

As if labor might happen on a runway,
birth fall out of a luggage cart.
Flames for the bright white anger
I rarely attain. Flames for the spent love
that brushes my kitchen ceiling
leaving the peeling paint untouched.

The Place

How did we get here? My ankle in your hand,
your mouth moving towards my mouth.
There is no one way to touch this.
Once in a moment of bravado you jumped up
from the bed and pressed me
to write it all down. *Don't change my name*
you said, like a drowning sailor who knows
it's too late to be rescued.

I let myself enjoy your long fingers
moving into the back of my neck.
Your left hand holds
the wheel of the car that guides us
through D.C.'s streets searching for cul de sacs
and dead ends. It is the search
for the world we wanted,
a scent of storm dust, of evening flower.
The place far from every day
that we bring to each other.

Only infrequent memory is ours.
I've known you since
sixteen, before you married
the woman you love whose image
will soon beckon you home,
leave me to write it all down
as if love in this world is a word problem
where the figures are true, the answer constant,
as in the equation for the rest of our lives.

MUTED GOLD

THE SCENT OF GASOLINE

As a child I'd inhale deeply the scent of gasoline,
open the back seat window and lift my chin to the wind.

My life shone with petroleum products:
paint thinner, shoe polish, amber jars of shellac.

High test my father would order
and while we checked the mileage chart

fumes would enter our bodies, the lightness
burnishing our capillaries,

investing us with longing
for *Rhode Island, Maine, Vermont.*

For my birthday I asked for a sky blue bottle
of cologne, *Eau de Esso;*

but instead he brought me smoky gray glasses,
oven-ware plastic tubs, the *limited time offer* of nostalgia.

What I needed was a burning sense across my skin,
gas stains on my scarf.

•

In Gaza City, I found excuses
to frequent the "Gas Palace," the chrome pillars

rinsed in florescent greens and shades of blue.
I loved to watch the arched pumps with their reckless

slot machine eyes, their loaded guns.
My friend Ámjad would fill the tank and sing a little to himself—

greet the employees smoking cigarettes
and fixing cars; men who worked extra hours,

their bodies like scraps of metal
taking their place among the stars.

I sent my father postcards edged in lighter fluid,
Greetings from Gaza no Quaker State, no bars.

•

Why mythologize bitter coffee
and squalid rest rooms?

BP for Niger, Senegal, and Mali.
I'd ride my mobilette up to the island,

uncap the tank. And more often times
than not, the sweet liquid would overflow

onto the body of my bike, splash
the braceleted knobs of my wrists,

and give the attendant and me
a soft rag of conversation.

A filling station. A place to go
to get filled up.

•

I miss the flying horse,
the nether worlds of *Gulf* and *Texaco*.

I miss the road maps, key chains, *Rubbermaid* cups;
the belief blossoming behind the words *fill 'er up.*

My father's world is gone now,
his body returning to the oil fields underground.

And to conjure him I breathe in
the dangerous, clock the miles to the gallon

before the needle stops traveling backward—falls
unencumbered, empty, lost.

SEAT MATE

I hate the way the inside of his nostrils twitch.
How they open wider as he leans forward,
holding the ice cream treat—his *Its-It*
in two plump swelling hands;
his short thick fingers curving to catch the drips.
He hunches his shoulders
and his square neck disappears—
all of his face falling deep into vanilla cream.
I am moved by my seat mate;
the way he flosses his teeth
in front of me. I'd like to
shoot this man, his veined and hairy
legs, his right arm exploding
over to my side of the seat.
I hear kissing noises
as he cleans his mouth with *Listerine,*
spits it into a paper cup.
He sports a stained multicolored jacket
on our flight from Boston to St. Paul.
How can I hate so readily
a man I don't even know?
Despise the elbow that jabs me regularly,
loathe the cloying way he keeps attempting conversation,
alternately talking to himself and then,
the video screen above our heads.
He wipes his mouth with a magazine,
seems to enjoy the friction it creates.
And by now I am fascinated with his ways.
How he pushes silver aviator glasses
up the slide of his nose. Hums as if
he's almost happy. And what is it he sees
sitting next to him? A woman in leather jacket
and jeans scratching notes in judgment of a stranger?

What does it mean to hate so readily? To burn with it?
The crumbs in his crotch, the bright pink skin,
a gold plated medallion and matching ring.
Is there any way to love
his body, to shift my shoulder on to the center
armrest, lean into his sleeve and say
"So where did you start today? Connecticut?
Vermont?" Our conversation would wander
until I could meet his gaze
unrevulsed. I'd smile into his blue-gray eyes,
touch his salt and pepper hair,
and put everything else behind us, clear away.
But I can't. Instead, I am silent as we cross
mountains, wheat fields, waterways. While Warren Beatty
tangos Annette Benning on some Technicolor island.
And when we de-plane I pray he's not headed for gate C3.
I move purposefully, knowing it is pitiful to be elated;
so pathetic to think I'm free.

GREEN STREET GRILL: FIRST DATE

During the silence
I look down at the table,
see our hands and the hook
of the umbrella's handle,
bent to form a question mark,
a set place to hold on to.
I turn away not wanting to notice
the frailness of collective fingers,
the unanimous plea to be touched.
For one moment all four hands seem brilliant
as stones that live in sea water—
our wrists exposed, calling
like an empty beach.

It's over so quickly
I can't tell if you've seen
me watching, trying to decipher
if our hands could reach—
clasp themselves dangerously
inside each other.
Or should the palms' imbedded heart lines
vote against contact,
choose to remain uncharted,
resplendent as the separate bodies
at this restaurant tonight;
the umbrella swaying on the table's edge,
waiting to comply with the weather.

1959

The year I was born my mother ate nothing but oranges,
sat in her bedroom in the sweet July heat and listened

as the world unfolded; turned the radio dial as Fidel captured
Santa Clara, Singapore became self-governing.

My father would return home for supper, the faint scent
of Cuban cigars on his kiss and she'd recount for him

the story of their days: *the Dalai Lama has left Tibet for Lhasa,*
or *Anne Frank's become a Broadway play.*

When my father lifts the sun spangled fruit from her hand,
he says, *Dear, don't worry. Our daughter will be old as Alaska,*

young as the islands of Hawaii. A toast to our daughter
he proclaims *may she peel the skin from this schizophrenic age.*

Lines Written Before Seeing an Ex-Lover Who Has Become a Sex Therapist Instead of a Mathematician

She's curious what advice
he gives his clients
whether she should request
a consultant's fee

for teaching him to knead
her neck and shoulders,
for leading guided walks
underneath her breasts, her hips, her chin.

What do you say to an ex-lover
now specializing
in cajoling sweet fevers
from other peoples' limbs—

pass the butter please,
how do you like your fish?
Dinner conversation may drift
to a lexicon of innuendo

or surprise; a marlin filet
mistaken for a shirt
of crêpe de Chine.
Will she let herself

evoke their first seduction
over strawberries and tea,
his summer-colored body
eager for the lessons

she promised
in advanced geometry?
They'll postulate theorems
in concentric circles,

polygons, and trapezoids,
coordinate arcs
and draw right angles
along perpendicular,

and then parallel sides.
Does he ever use her
as a text book illustration
of *unproven symmetry?*

Or in stressing *sexual*
misconduct among tutors of the *GRE?*
He'll check his watch, apologize,
an appointment he must keep.

But in the garage they'll linger
by rectangles of *Honda, Camaro, Jeep.*
And when they finally kiss,
his mouth urgent and deep,

she'll greet the radius of his tongue,
finger the slope of his thigh. And wiser now,
she'll keep to her belief in independent lines;
and mouth the words *good-night.*

THE EXACT MOMENT

Our fingers apprised of the situation begin to flirt and flicker across the table.
Your slope of thigh leans hard against my thigh, constructs a temporary shelter,

propagates a startling need in me. Is love just a fixed point in the brain,
encoded chemicals that click into place? You construct a scaffold of syntax,

sensual measures of sestets and pantoums; direct and probe
love's rhythmic equations with erotic pluck, listen with all your body,

enamored with the scene; this lip of precipice. Here, unencumbered
in a New England barn I locate my pulse and realize it's no longer my own.

As we walk out at night our flashlights aim above the falling snow
into a reach of sky. *To think it never ends* you say, betraying

the longing hidden in astronomy. The eloquence of light
snagged on matter. When you say, *there's a lifetime of traveling*

between ourselves and the stars. I know you will leave, abandon this
for your other life. And in this exact moment, before what is unattainable

overwhelms us is when I want you. Will take you and wrestle limb over limb
on the edge of the snow covered road. For once do it right—and in doing

shape this desire; mix infinity with red wine and the taste of the body
arcing us into one like a constellation that hangs

by invincible cords in the night, already dead and blazing,
without sound, without insight.

MEN AT WORK

All summer long men appear
eye level with my kitchen table. Through my window I watch
men across the road on rooftops. It is impossible to know

what they're trying to do. Red and blue wheelbarrows
roll across the roof. Some men in suspenders, one bare chested, men
with headbands and tattoos move dirt from one rooftop

to the next. Men moving back and forth carrying shovels
in their arms, taking away branches chopped off the only tree
on my street. Men going to the edge and looking down.

So quiet in their blue and red and flesh colored
T-shirts. I am a voyeur, delighting from across the street
in men's muscular arms and legs rhythmic

in their vaudeville procrastination. The one with the yellow
knee pads tied with kite string around his trousers has been
to all corners of the rooftop. He carts his

load from front to back, finally abandoning it
to shimmy over to the next roof. And as if predetermined,
the action is suddenly broken, the men stay where they are.

One takes an orange from his pocket, another strikes a match,
someone bites a coffee cake and now
they can begin to talk.

EARLY MORNING WEATHER

The rain makes me conjure a lover
with slender hips, smooth as
driftwood branches, a woman

with nerve. Rainwater
courses my veins, rises
like perfumed steam

from my red tea kettle.
The water margin surges,
changes the scale—drenches cedar,

hemlock, mountain ash;
seduces them to grow.
Was I conceived in the rain?

In the sound of a train slowing
on wooden slats, dominoes tumbling,
the kick and click of it? Rainwater

washes down umbrella tops,
slips between the sheets,
seeds messages to an island

of porous desire. Can't you tell
that under a persimmon sky,
in one split of lightning this woman

will say *Yes!* affirm the slant
of the body, the human body,
fed on mud and winter sod, silver

cactus burrs, scented pine?
Rain spangles the light,
traces the play of what could be

your lips pressing to the confluence
of my thighs. Rainwater stands up
on rooftops, chimney pots, crosses

the sloping boundaries
of skin with rapt attention.
Rain on the window

breaking the echo of one empty heart
or is it the jazz pulse of the sky?
I open my blouse

to the rain, to the splash
and the sizzle—

jubilant in wet edge light.

WHAT I WILL TAKE FROM MY MOTHER

A blue glass jar of mismatched buttons,
silver snaps and peeling pearls.
Notions recycled from hand-me-down coats
shirt collars, cardigans, stoles.
I will take from her the gold leaf
on ceramic black machine
which stitched infrequent slips of cotton,
emergency hemlines, seams.
And from stuffed inside
the sewing machine chair,
I'll pocket bobbins of coral thread
and inherit grandmother's zig-zag scissors,
to create an unfrayed edge.
I'll copy the recipe for banana bread
with hot cinnamon-apple pears,
take scouring pads I used to scrub gold stars
imbedded in linoleum squares.
There's polished cutlery in graying plastic sacks;
photographs of cousins
from Lithuanian towns
who left in brown burlap bags.
I will tear the aged paper mural
from the attic of our house
a carbonized figure on horseback
racing towards one forty watt bulb.
What do we take? This and more—
a toaster, a blender, sharp attention
to closed closet doors.
My mother will nod as she passes, touch
her cheek, then hair. I'll smell the slight
musk of lipstick, the dust-caked air
moving as our figures, unanswered,
travel up the numinous stepladder stairs.

LAST BREATH

Breathe! I demanded, *like when you had your babies.*
You have to. And she did—considered the request,
paused in between to see if she had done it right,
to see if it was what she still wanted to do.
And for the first time in twenty-four hours
we knew she was still with us. She knew
she was where for the moment
she wanted to be. The book says ninety seconds
is how long a person can go without taking air—*breathe...*
a fact we'd learned that morning,
came equipped to her bed
with second hands on our watches.

It was Friday evening, the beginning of Shabbat.
C'mon, like this. Pull the air into you,
like when we swim.
My Dad, my sister, and the night nurse
who'd never had anyone die on her shift—
we laughed and shouted on the edge of hysteria
as my mother matched her breath with my own.
The sound turning labored, then restful,
like a rip tide temporarily at ease.

She can hear us! She heard you!
As if her body had left us one last sense
which we'd almost overlooked.
Breathe with me.
Fifty-six..., eighty-one..., ninety-five...one hundred and twenty
Breathe...
How could she have forgotten, after the ins and outs of her life?
But I was showing her,
with exaggerated sighs, shouts. *Breathe!*
—/

And then nothing more.
Just a body in a room.
The rented wheelchair moved against the wall.
Morphine to pour down the toilet, a paper to sign.
—/
Cover the mirror, remove all rings
and earrings, nothing other-worldly at all.
Breathe, keep her corpse company for the night.
Breathe, it's up to you to keep her alive.

1 JANUARY 1999

Everything is still
possible. Each
ordinary thing appears
as new: a tall blue vase,
a Spanish teacup, chipped—
the shadows your shoes made at noon.

Today, before resolution wavers,
freezes along the drainpipes, evaporates to
almost...could have been...soon...
Before the predictable falls back
through the crack of dinner plates,
to the blender's chromatic beat,

under the throat of longing
too deep to exhume—
there is this chance to disinherit
        the thousand permutations
of *to lose*: erase the misplaced heart,
the body's elopement, the day
undressed by a mountain ruin.

        In abeyance
the penultimate year is light,
radiant as blue water, improved.
This is the moment for promises
unbroken. A postcard sent,
some angel cake, clean curtains
to show off the view.

Here in my kitchen,
among the spatulas and colanders,
silver tins and one wooden spoon

I refuse the year's migration,
remain fixed in the not-yet of
things, memory a giveaway box,
tomorrow still unproven.

      In this moment
between the moments, it is
the parentheses that preoccupy me;
the air that bridges the complete
to the incomplete—
the time your fingertips adored me
to the time your feet got up to leave.

EDGE LIGHT

Florence, Oregon

Rock cliffs of Florence, storm light of beach and sky,
salt wash of tide, the curve of white shoulders,

wind spray of damp and delight;
of possibility churning and returning

merely to please itself again.

I watch the late afternoon cast out its blue signals
collect them as two shore birds configure,

change places, dive ungoverned
into the spill of waves.

•

The unmasked claim of the body.

The persistence of skin
as it deciphers, anticipates, holds

back from another; another angle
of hips, turn of fingertips, pull of breasts.

Why does desire arc?

Why does the physical assert itself
simply to withdraw such light again?

•

Caught in the slippage

where the moon returns tide prints to land;
sandpipers chart the shoreline

in a gesture first whimsical,
then ink dark.

Balancers of the visible

the birds cross-hatch the margins—
ironic, elliptical, in full range.

●

Silver wings trapped by light—

a causeway of wings:
singular, shining, rare

in need of water, of flight,
transparent cries

between the floating borders of terror and air.

●

The shoreline seduction, the mirror, the claim.

The implacable shimmer of silver coins on the sea
of a moment moving closer, further back

before its over, re-patterned,
lost and released.

An arc of edge light, sheaf of memory,
cloud line disappearing.

LOVE IN THE TIME OF AIDS

You are afraid
of a moist toothbrush, disposable razor,
fearful of the inside
of your lover's mouth.
Too terrified to pose an inquiry in shorthand
positive,   negative?
You imagine your date's response
I don't know.
Remembering the scent of one man
the fingertips of another
triggers the inevitable moment
when your eyes
search this new body,   stop
and check for signs—
like a pilot before the flight
records temperature and distance
knowing even this cannot ensure a safe journey.

The lovers he's had before
are now your lovers
and yours are his
their health and habits as migratory
as your own blood.

In the morning
you telephone for the test
anonymously. No way to study or plan.
The voice at the end of the line
gives you the number you will use
as your identity, sets a time and place
where you meet a man named Manuel.
No hint of this, no mark
will mar your records.

You bargain with yourself.
You'll give up kissing—
no more dancing
of tongues. You promise to become
a condom connoisseur. Take six-month tests
for HIV as if they were multiple choice.
As if the pilot knows whether or not the plane
will crash or glide across the sky,
as if the sky knows what is written underneath its skin.

ALL THAT WE NEED, 4 A.M.

Cape Town, South Africa

The train threads a needle through the night,
pulls the weight of wind, of ostriches and coal;
stitches up the empty pockets of small towns,
the edge line of cities. And the whistle releases an echo
of the psalms, a long cry along the Indian coast,
gathering past it stations of sorrow: a sensual song.

The sparks of light on a quiet street,
a vision that occurs regularly, only to leave,
which brings with it Wagner: short – short, long—
until music reaches past the heart's chambers,
gives way, and lovers sigh, turn over,
too full of light to sleep.

MUTED GOLD

My father died just as my plane touched down.
He taught me journeys don't happen in straight lines.
I loved him without ever needing words.
Is memory a chain of alibis?

He taught me journeys don't happen in straight lines.
His father sailed Odessa to Boston Harbor.
Is memory a chain of alibis?
The story I choose a net of my own desires?

His father sailed Odessa to Boston Harbor.
Dad worked beside him in their corner store.
The story I choose a net of my own desires?
I wish I'd known to ask the simple questions.

Dad worked beside him in their corner store.
They shelved the tins of black beans, fruit preserves, and almond cakes.
I wish I'd known to ask the simple questions,
he'd have stayed with me and gossiped over toast.

They shelved the tins of black beans, fruit preserves and almond cakes.
What colors did they wear, what languages were spoken?
He'd have stayed with me and gossiped over toast,
now he's smiling but I can't summon the thoughts he's thinking.

What colors did they wear, what languages were spoken?
Was it a muted gold, a world of shattered feeling?
Now he's smiling but I can't summon the thoughts he's thinking.
I pack his clothes away, mark them *for Goodwill*.

Was it a muted gold, a world of shattered feeling?
What good will it do to dwell, I hear him say.
I pack his clothes away, mark them *for Goodwill.*
but I hold fast to one old T-shirt, butter-smooth, and brilliant.

What good will it do to dwell, I hear him say.
He much preferred to glide along life's surface.
But I hold fast to one old T-shirt, butter-smooth, and brilliant
and tell a story by moonlight, to try and keep him with me.

He much preferred to glide along life's surface.
I love him now with images, with words,
and tell a story by moonlight, to try and keep him with me.
My father died just as my plane touched down.

Take Off

From one dot
on the map
to the other
the airplane clocks

a reassuring distance
up and over
lakes, countries,
across the ambitious lines

of time zones;
smoothly along its own trajectory
it travels—confidently
into other hemispheres.

Suspended
alone in this fuchsia sky
the ephemeral becomes
the real, thinking

temporarily wiser.
And I begin to see my life working
like a gyroscope

increasing in power
as I detach from regret
and fly incrementally
towards fire.

NOTES AND DEDICATIONS

The Woman with a Hole in the Middle of Her Face: tsadakah is defined as both charity and justice in the Arabic, Hausa, and Hebrew languages.

Sarajevo: the Sarajevo Rose is the pattern made by a shell exploding, in this case the imprint is left on the tarmac.

Oslobodjenje: Oslobodjenje, Sarajevo's independent newspaper published everyday during the three and a half years of the Bosninan war. *Oslobodjenje's* offices were targeted and set alight by Serbian forces during the first three months of the seige. The poem is inspired by an interview with Kemal Kurspahic published in the *American Scholar,* spring 1998.

Nocturne: How will this country answer you? is inspired by the line "is this how this country is going to answer you?" from "Arrival at Santos" by Elizabeth Bishop from *Complete Poems 1927-1979.* *Songololo* is a South African word for centipede, origin unknown. A *lamed-vav tzaddik* in the Kabbalistic tradition, is one of the thirty-six hidden saints who quietly do their work in the world in a way that holds the universe together.

Whatever Happened to the Bodies... is based upon a National Public Radio story which aired on March 10, 1996 and began, "This evening we bring you a report about an unusual, grim, and sacred perspective on the recent bombings. We join the volunteers who help clean up the carnage. Jewish law states it's a special Mitzvah to bring a body, to bury it whole, to give it the best respect."

On Photographing the National Library: on August 25, 1992, the Bosnian Serb army continually bombed the National Library with

incendiary shells destroying the largest repository of Bosnian history—
the intent of the attack. Karadzic then accused the Bosnian Muslims
of blowing up their own archive in order to make the Serbs look bad to
the international press.

Taoseño: The Morada is a dwelling place where God has pitched his
tent; the church of the Moradians.

Dedications:

Haiti is for Yves-Rose Saintdic.
La Verbena Cemetery is for Giovanni Soto.
Nocturne is for Will Berkovitz.
Taoseño is for Mark Cohen.
The Exact Moment and *Stories* are for Peter Wallace.
The Scent of Gasoline and *Muted Gold* are in memory of Abraham Rich.
Last Breath and *What I Will Take from My Mother* are in memory of
Lillian Rich.

Susan Rich recently completed a Fulbright Fellowship to research poetry and human rights in South Africa. Her poems have appeared in journals and magazines including *DoubleTake, Harvard Magazine, Poet Lore and The Massachusetts Review.* She has served as an electoral monitor in Bosnia, human rights educator in Gaza, writer-in-residence in Zimbabwe, a Peace Corps Volunteer in Niger, West Africa and a Program Coordinator for Amnesty International USA. Her awards include fellowships and grants from the Blue Mountain Center, The Cottages at Hedgebrook, Millay Colony for the Arts, and Fundacion Valaparasio. She currently lives in the Pacific Northwest and teaches global studies and writing at Highline College.

Author photo: Bob Walter

American Poetry from White Pine Press

THE WAY BACK
Wyn Cooper
4 pages $14.00 paper

THE CARTOGRAPHER'S TONGUE
Susan Rich
108 pages $14.00 paper

TROUBLE IN HISTORY
David Keller
94 pages $14.00 paper
Winner 1999 White Pine Press Poetry Prize

THE FLOATING ISLAND
Pablo Medina
104 pages $14.00 paper

WINGED INSECTS
Joel Long
96 pages $14.00 paper
Winner 1998 White Pine Press Poetry Prize

IN THE PINES: LOST POEMS 1972-1997
David St. John
224 pages $16.00 paper

A GATHERING OF MOTHER TONGUES
Jacqueline Joan Johnson
116 pages $12.00 paper
Winner 1997 White Pine Press Poetry Prize

PRETTY HAPPY!
Peter Johnson
96 pages $12.00 paper

BODILY COURSE
Deborah Gorlin
90 pages $12.00 paper
Winner 1996 White Pine Press Poetry Prize

TREEHOUSE: NEW & SELECTED POEMS
William Kloefkorn
224 pages $15.00 paper

JUMPING OUT OF BED
Robert Bly
48 pages $7.00 paper

WHY NOT
Joel Oppenheimer
46 pages $7.00 paper

TWO CITIZENS
James Wright
48 pages $8.00 paper

SLEEK FOR THE LONG FLIGHT
William Matthews
80 pages $8.00 paper
WHY I CAME TO JUDEVINE
David Budbill
72 pages $7.00 paper

AZUBAH NYE
Lyle Glazier
56 pages $7.00 paper

SMELL OF EARTH AND CLAY
East Greenland Eskimo Songs
38 pages $5.00 paper

FINE CHINA: TWENTY YEARS OF EARTH'S DAUGHTERS
230 pages $14.00 paper

CERTAINTY
David Romtvedt
96 pages $12.00 paper

ZOO & CATHEDRAL
Nancy Johnson
80 pages $12.00 paper
Winner 1995 White Pine Press Poetry Prize

DESTINATION ZERO
Sam Hamill
184 pages $15.00 paper
184 pages $25.00 cloth

CLANS OF MANY NATIONS
Peter Blue Cloud
128 pages $14.00 paper

HEARTBEAT GEOGRAPHY
John Brandi
256 pages $15.00 paper

LEAVING EGYPT
Gene Zeiger
80 pages $12.00 paper

WATCH FIRE
Christopher Merrill
192 pages $14.00 paper

BETWEEN TWO RIVERS
Maurice Kenny
168 pages $12.00 paper

TEKONWATONTI: MOLLY BRANT
Maurice Kenny

DRINKING THE TIN CUP DRY
William Kloefkorn
87 pages $8.00 paper

GOING OUT, COMING BACK
William Kloefkorn
96 pages $11.00 paper

POETRY IN TRANSLATION FROM WHITE PINE PRESS

THE CITY AND THE CHILD
Ales Debeljak
68 pages $14.00

PERCHED ON NOTHING'S BRANCH
Selected Poems of Attila Joszef
104 pages $14.00

WINDOWS THAT OPEN INWARD
Poems by Pablo Neruda, Photographs by Milton rogovin
96 pages $20.00

HEART OF DARKNESS
Ferida Durakovic
112 pages $14.00

AN ABSENCE OF SHADOWS
Marjorie Agosin
128 pages $15.00

HEART'S AGONY
SELECTED POEMS OF CHIHA KIM
128 PAGES $14.00

THE FOUR QUESTIONS OF MELANCHOLY
Tomaz Salamun
224 pages $15.00

A GABRIELA MISTRAL READER
232 pages $15.00

ALFONSINA STORNI: SELECTED POEMS
72 pages $8.00

CIRCLES OF MADNESS: MOTHERS OF THE PLAZA DE MAYO
Marjorie Agosin
128 pages $13.00   Bilingual

SARGASSO
Marjorie Agosin
92 pages $12.00   Bilingual